Elementary Swordplay and Broadsword-play

Compiled by Victor Wu

HAI FENG PUBLISHING COMPANY
HONG KONG

First Edition 1983

Published by
Hai Feng Publishing Co., Ltd.
Rm. 1503 Wing On House,
71 Des Voeux Rd. C., Hong Kong.

Printed by
Friendly Printing Co., Ltd.
Flat B1, 3/F., Luen Ming Hing Ind. Bldg.,
36 Muk Cheong Street, Tokwawan,
Kowloon, H.K.

Distributed by
China International Book Trading Corporation
(GUOJI SHUDIAN)
P.O. Box 399, Beijing, China

Printed in Hong Kong

初級刀劍術

中華人民共和國 編
體育運動委員會

海峰出版社有限公司 出版
（香港德輔道中71號永安集團大廈1503室）

友利印刷有限公司印刷
（香港九龍土瓜灣木廠街36號4樓B1座）

中國國際圖書貿易總公司發行
（中國國際書店）
北京399信箱

1988年（報紙本）第一版
編號：（英文版）
ISBN 962-238-026-3
HF-44-P
T-E-2239P

Contents

Chapter One: Elementary Swordplay   1
   1. List of Forms   2
   2. Instruction on Techniques   5

Chapter Two: Elementary Broadsword-Play   61
   1. List of Forms   62
   2. Instruction on Techniques   65

Chapter One
ELEMENTARY SWORDPLAY

1. List of Forms

Opening Stance

Stage One

1. Straight Thrust with Bow Step
2. Back Cut
3. Side Cut with Bow Step
4. Left Stroke with Bow Step
5. Horizontal Cut with Knee Raised
6. Lower Back Thrust
7. Swing Up and Straight Thrust
8. Raise Sword Horizontally with Hollow Step

Stage Two

1. Horizontal Cut with Hollow Step
2. Chop with Bow Step
3. Tap Forward with Sword
4. Parry Below with Knee Raised
5. Straight Thrust with Knee Raised
6. Back Horizontal Stroke
7. Chop with Cross-Legged Crouch
8. Lower Tap with Knee Raised

Stage Three

1. Straight Thrust with Feet Together
2. Raise Sword with Bow Step
3. Chop with Cross-Legged Crouch
4. Reinforce Wrist (Right)

5. Reinforce Wrist (Left)
6. Hop and Flip
7. Press Down with Side Crouch
8. Straight Thrust with Knee Raised

Stage Four
1. Side Cut with Bow Step
2. Back Cut
3. Flip with Cross-Legged Crouch
4. Side Cut with Bow Step
5. Step Up with Left Cut
6. Step Up with Right Cut
7. Back Cut with Cross-Legged Squat
8. Horizontal Swirl

Closing Stance

— # 2. Instruction on Techniques

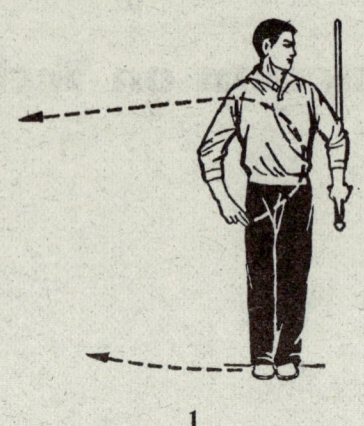

1

Opening Stance

Stand erect with feet closed. Hold sword by the cross-piece in left hand with thumb on one side, forefinger in middle, lengthwise on handle, and the other three fingers on the other side; the whole cross-piece rests in hollow of hand with the blade behind forearm, pointing up. Right hand forms the pointing fingers, i.e., with forefinger and middle finger stretched together, the other two closed in hollow of hand, and thumb over the nail of the fourth finger; wrist is turned up with knuckles upward, and fore- and middle fingers pointing down to left. Both arms are hanging with elbows slightly tucked up. Eyes looking to the left horizontally. (Fig. 1)

Remember: When holding sword, the blade should be held close to forearm, perpendicular to ground. Both shoulders are relaxed with chest out, belly in, and both legs straight erect.

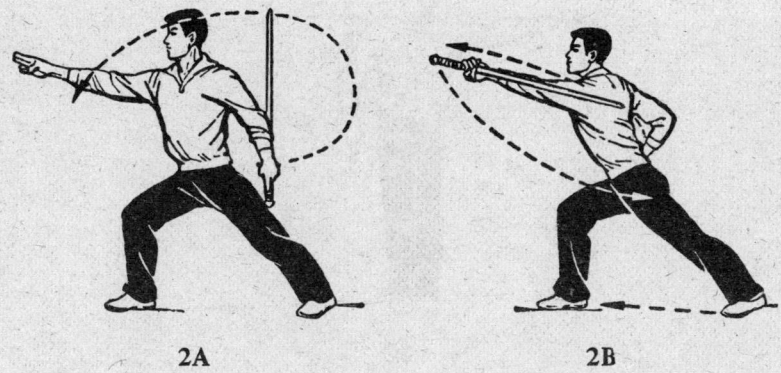

2A   2B

Form 1

1. Torso turns half to right, and right foot takes a step to right, bending knee; left heel turns out on ball of foot with leg stretched, forming a right bow step. As right foot steps aside, right pointing fingers are raised with elbow crooked, passing before chest and left shoulder, ending stretched horizontally to right, thumb on top. Eyes on pointing fingers. (Fig. 2A)
2. Torso turns right. Left hand holding sword is raised extended, passing overhead in an arc to right and ends in front of body with thumb down and arm turned over and extended at shoulder level; right pointing fingers are drawn beside waist with elbow crooked and hollow of hand upward. (Fig. 2B)

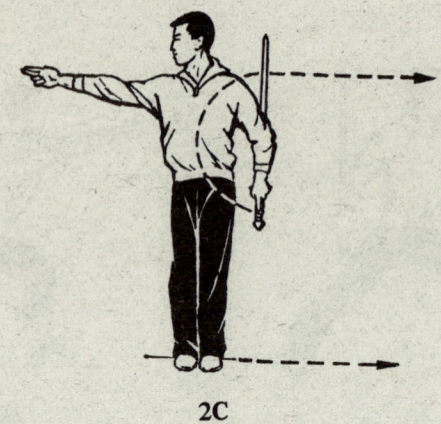

2C

3. Left foot moves beside the right. Left hand holding sword drops hanging on left side; right pointing fingers point to right with arm extended horizontally, thumb up. Eyes on pointing fingers. (Fig. 2C)

Remember: The three movements above must be well linked up. Both shoulders should be relaxed. While drawing an arc with sword in hand, left arm should be raised straight up, and torso should turn right without shifting feet. While left arm is swung to shoulder level, elbow should be slightly bent to allow right pointing fingers to come above back of left hand, pointing up. When left arm is dropped, sword should be held perpendicular to ground, pointing upward.

3A   3B

Form 2
1. Left foot takes a step to left, bending knee; right heel turns out on ball of foot with leg stretched, forming a left bow step. Torso turns left. As left foot steps aside, left hand holding sword is raised with arm crooked before chest in an arc and extended to left with thumb down. (Fig. 3A)
2. Left leg stands erect, and right foot comes forward beside the left. Left hand holding sword drops beside body; right pointing fingers comes forward from behind ear with elbow bent and points straight forward extended with fore-finger on top, eyes on pointing fingers. (Fig. 3B)

Remember: While pointing out, elbow should be fully extended with finger tips a bit higher than shoulder.

4A   4B

Form 3
1. Left hand holding sword is extended forward, thumb down, over right pointing fingers. Right pointing fingers are drawn under left arm with elbow bent before left shoulder, pointing up. Torso turns right, and right foot takes a step to right, bending knee, and left leg stretches taut with toes turned in, forming a right bow step. Eyes looking left. (Fig. 4A)
2. Torso turns right, and right fingers pass before body and point horizontally to right extended, forefinger on top. Eyes on pointing fingers. (Fig. 4B)

Remember: In bow step, left leg should be stretched taut, with soles of both feet well set on ground. Torso is inclined forward with chest out and back arched. Left hand holding sword is extended with shoulder relaxed.

5

Form 4

Ball of right foot turns in, and torso turns left, shifting weight on right leg; left foot draws back half a step, bending knee with ball of foot on ground, forming a left hollow step. While left foot is shifting, left hand holding sword is drawn before chest with elbow bent and hollow of hand facing out; right fingers are also drawn before chest with elbow bent and hollow of hand facing in, ready to take over sword from left hand. Eyes on sword point. (Fig. 5)

Remember: In the hollow step, weight must be fully rested on right leg with heel on ground. Chest should be thrown out and back arched and slightly inclined forward. Elbows should be kept level, with sword point slightly higher than left elbow.

6

Stage One

Form 1   Straight Thrust with Bow Step

Now right hand takes over sword from the left, and the left is closed to form pointing fingers. Left foot takes half a step forward, bending knee; right heel turns out on ball of foot with leg stretched, forming a left bow step. Meanwhile, torso turns left, and right hand holding sword thrusts straight forward with thumb on top; left pointing fingers are extended horizontally backward with forefinger on top. Eyes on sword point. (Fig. 6)

Remember: In a bow step, the leg in front should bend at knee with thigh level, and both feet should be set square on ground. Torso should be inclined slightly forward, waist turned left and back arched without jutting out buttocks. Both shoulders are relaxed with the right swung forward and the left back. Sword point is kept slightly higher than shoulder.

7

Form 2   Back Cut

Left leg is straightened without shifting foot; right foot takes a step forward, bending knee slightly, and torso turns right. Meanwhile, right hand holding sword swings up and cuts backward with blade at shoulder level, thumb on top; left pointing fingers go down and come up in front in an arc, ending raised above head with elbow bent and thumb down. Eyes on sword point. (Fig. 7)

Remember: The movements above must be well linked and coordinated. On turning, waist should be twisted right without shifting left foot. Blade must be in line with arm.

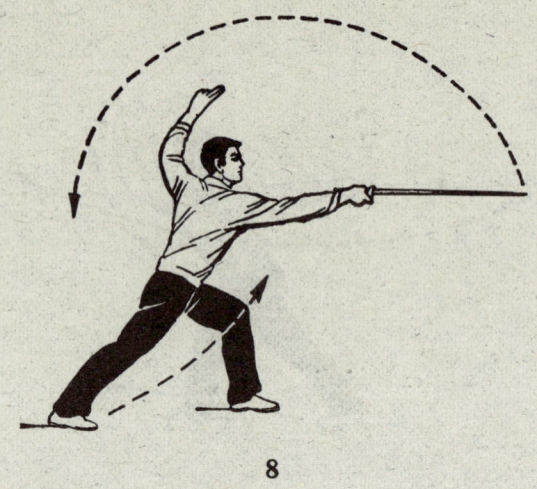

8

Form 3   Side Cut with Bow Step

Left foot takes a step forward obliquely to left, bending knee; right leg stretches taut with toes turned in, forming a left bow step. Meanwhile, left pointing fingers come down before chest before going up in an arc, ending raised above head with elbow bent, thumb down; right hand holding sword (hollow facing up) cuts horizontally forward, with point of sword pointing slightly to right. Eyes looking forward. (Fig. 8)

Remember: While cutting, keep wrist soft.

9A

Form 4   Left Stroke with Bow Step

1. Torso turns left, and right knee is drawn up in front with toes down and back of foot perpendicular to ground. Meanwhile, right hand holding sword twists clockwise, swinging sword up and back in an arc, ending with elbow bent, wrist and forearm against abdomen, hollow of hand facing in; left fingers then drop upon right wrist, hollow facing down. Eyes on blade. (Fig. 9A)

9B

2. Right foot lands in front obliquely to right, bending knee; left leg stretches taut with toes turned in, forming a right bow step. Meanwhile, right hand holding sword goes down and forward backhand with small finger on top; left fingers follow right hand by supporting its wrist. Eyes on sword point. (Fig. 9B)

Remember: The movement of sword either backward or forward must be coordinated with raising knee or landing foot, and the sword should not be held too tight. When the bow step is set, torso is inclined slightly forward with back straight, buttocks in, and sword point slightly lower than pointing fingers.

10

Form 5   Horizontal Cut with Knee Raised

Left foot takes a step forward, and right wrist turns up facing obliquely left with arm bent, swinging sword left and over head before right foot is raised in front with knee bent. Right wrist goes on turning so that sword comes to right and back with hollow of hand turned up, and cuts forward; left finger go to left and up in an arc, and is raised over head with elbow bent. Eyes looking forward. (Fig. 10)

Remember: When sword swings from left to right, torso must lean back so as to allow sword pass over face and not over top of head. In raising right leg, the left must stand firm and erect whereas right knee should go as high as possible, to cover groin with foot. Torso is inclined slightly forward, with chest out and abdomen in.

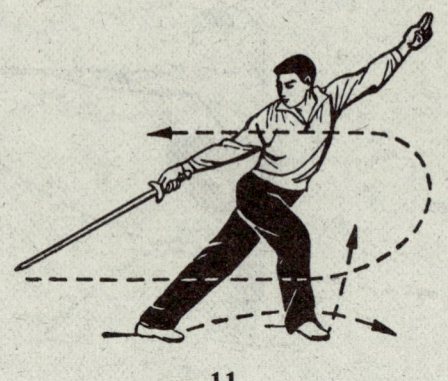

11

Form 6　Lower Back Thrust

　　Right foot lands in front with toes turned out, bending knee torso turns right. Meanwhile, right hand holding sword turns wrist back, pointing sword down, and thrusts back below with sword-point lower than knee and thumb on top; left fingers at first come close to right hand and, while sword thrusts forward, goes up, forward fully extended with forefinger on top. Eyes on sword-point. (Fig. 11)
Remember: Right hand holding sword must be drawn before body with arm bent, and while right foot lands in front and torso turns right, thrusts out with force. Left leg is straightened whereas the right is slightly bent with waist turned right, and pointing fingers are in line with sword.

12A   12B

Form 7   Swing Up and Straight Thrust
1. Left foot takes a step forward, with knee slightly crouched, and right hand turns thumb down and, with a flick of wrist, swings sword point left and up until it is before left shoulder, holding sword horizontally before chest with elbow bent and hollow of hand facing in; meanwhile, left leg stands erect with right knee drawn up, and left fingers are on right wrist. (Fig. 12A)
2. Torso immediately turns right on ball of left foot, and right hand plunges sword down with left fingers supporting wrist. Eyes on sword point. (Fig. 12B)

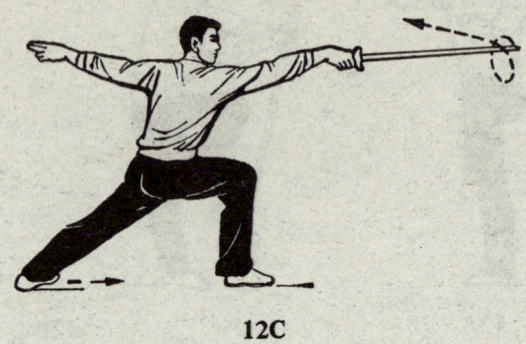

12C

3. Left leg again turns on ball of foot as right foot takes a big step back, bending knee, and torso turns about clockwise with left leg stretched, toes in, forming a right bow step. Meanwhile, right hand holding sword thrusts forward with sword point at shoulder level and thumb up. Eyes on sword point. (Fig. 12C)

Remember: The swing-up, plunge-down and forward thrust should be well linked up and coordinated with footwork while thrusting both feet should be set square on ground with torso inclined slightly forward, chest out and back arched.

13A

Form 8   Raise Sword Horizontally with Hollow Step
1. Right hand holding sword first draws a small circle anti-clockwise with sword point, turning thumb down. Meanwhile, torso turns about clockwise on right heel and ball of left foot with right toes turned out, and left foot takes half a step forward with both knees slightly bent, forming a cross step. While turning body, right hand holding, sword with thumb down, draws it up backward with elbow bent, raising it horizontally overhead, left fingers pass before shoulder and rest upon right wrist. Eyes looking left horizontally. (Fig. 13A)

13B

2. Right leg bends at knee without shifting, and left foot takes a step forward, bending knee slightly with ball of foot barely touching ground, while weight is shifted on right leg, forming a left hollow step. As right hand draws back, left fingers extend straight forward with hollow of hand facing down. Eyes on pointing fingers. (Fig. 13B)

Remember: Weight must be fully rested on right leg, and right elbow is slightly crooked so that sword remains horizontal above forehead whereas left arm is fully extended with fingers a little above shoulder.

14

Stage Two

Form 1   Horizontal Cut with Hollow Step

Right heel turns outward, and torso turns right shifting weight onto left leg, as right heel is raised up with only ball of foot on ground, forming a right hollow step. While turning body, right hand cuts down horizontally with thumb on top; left pointing fingers are raised with elbow bent and, hollow of hand facing upper left. Eyes on sword point. (Fig. 14)

15

Form 2   Chop with Bow Step

Right foot sets firm on ground, and shifts weight forward. Left fingers go under right armpit, and right arm twists counter-clockwise, turning hollow of hand downward. Left foot takes a step forward obliquely to left, bending knee; right leg is stretched taut with toes turned in, forming a left bow step. While left foot is stepping forward, right hand holding sword draws a small circle clockwise with a flick of wrist before chopping down with sword point at knee level; left pointing fingers come out left and upward in an arc, ending raised above head with elbow crooked. Torso is slightly inclined forward. Eyes on sword point. (Fig. 15)
Remember: While chopping, swing right shoulder forward and the left back, and sword point should be in line with hand and shoulder.

16A

Form 3   Tap Forward with Sword
1. Right foot steps up beside the left, with ball of foot on ground and both legs are partly crouched. Right hand turns wrist up, swinging sword point back beside ear with elbow slightly bent; left fingers then drop in front upon right wrist. Eyes looking to the right forward horizontally. (Fig. 16A)

16B

2. Following the preceding step, right foot leaps a step forward, dropping on the ground with knee half crouched; left foot follows up beside right foot with knee bent and toes on ground forming a "T" step. Meanwhile, right hand holding sword taps ahead with thumb on top; left pointing fingers are raised over head with elbow crooked and hollow of hand upward. Eyes on sword point. (Fig. 16B)

Remember: While tapping, right arm is extended forward with wrist bent down a little higher than shoulder and force concentrated on sword point, which is a little lower than hand. When left foot comes up, right thigh should be held level, and back of left foot is held taut with toes beside arch of right foot and both legs close together. Torso is inclined slightly forward with chest out, back straight.

17A   17B

Form 4   Parry below with Knee Raised
1. Right leg stretches straight as left foot takes a step back, bending knee, and torso leans back. Right arm turns outward with hollow facing upward, swinging sword to right and back upper in an arc; left pointing fingers remain in position. (Fig. 17A)
2. Right arm goes on to turn inward with hollow of hand downward, swinging sword to left and down in front in an arc to parry a blow, while torso is inclined forward with left knee raised. Eyes on sword point. (Fig. 17B)

Remember: The sword is in fact swung from left to right to complete a circle without break. Left knee should be drawn up as high as possible with back of foot taut; right leg stands firm erect. Right arm should be in line with sword, both inclined at the same angle.

18A

Form 5   Straight Thrust with Knee Raised
1. Right leg is partly bent at knee, and left foot lands in front with toes turned out. Right arm twists outward, turning hollow of hand upward and, as left foot lands, draws hand back before chest with elbow bent, hollow facing inward, and sword point at shoulder level: left pointing fingers drop down immediately to rest upon sword handle, with arm bent horizontally. Both legs are crossed, eyes are looking at sword point. (Fig. 18A)

18B

2. Right knee is drawn up in front with left leg standing erect. Right hand holding sword thrusts straight forward levelly, thumb on top; left fingers point backward extended, with hollow downward. Eyes on sword point. (Fig. 18B)

Remember: The holding of sword and landing of left foot as well as straight thrust and drawing up of knee must be well coordinated.

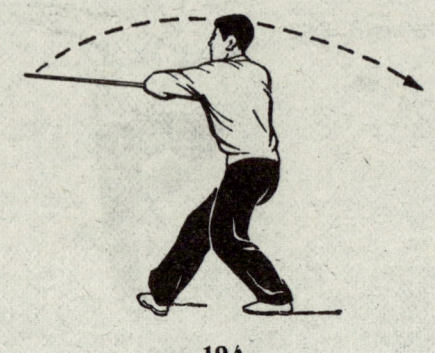

19A

Form 6   Back Horizontal Stroke
1. Right foot lands forward with toes turned outward; left foot turns heel outward on ball of foot, bending knee, while torso turns right, forming a cross step. Right arm revolves outward, turning hollow of hand up and draws sword back before chest with elbow bent, keeping blade in line with right shoulder; left fingers are raised with arm extended and then drop with elbow bent beside left ear to rest upon hollow of right hand. Eyes on sword point. (Fig. 19A)

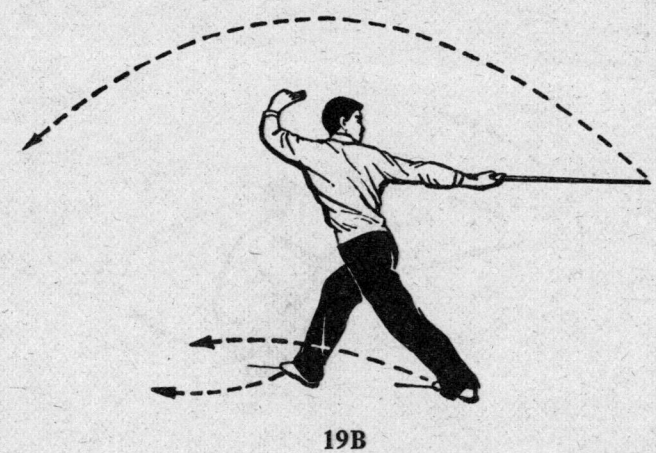

19B

2. Torso turns a bit further right with left leg stretched taut and right leg slightly bent. Meanwhile, right hand strikes heavily to right with sword horizontally, hollow of hand remaining upward; left pointing fingers are raised with elbow bent above the left upward of forehead. Eyes on sword point. (Fig. 19B)

Remember: The withdrawal of sword and striking back must be linked up. While striking the blow, force is concentrated on front part of sword; when the blow is struck, torso is swung right without shifting left foot.

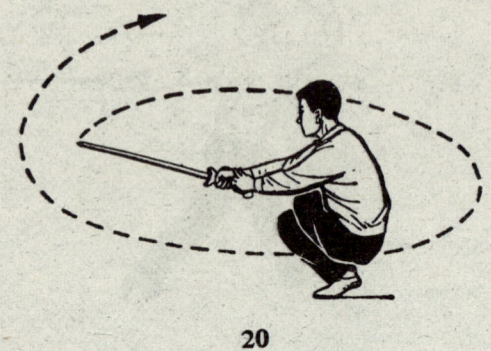

20

Form 7   Chop with Cross-Legged Crouch

Right foot kicks against the ground to jump up, and left foot follows by taking a step to left; as soon as it lands, right foot takes a side step behind the left, and both legs crouch crossed, left over right. While jumping, right hand raises sword and chops down when legs are crouched, with thumb on top and sword point at ankle level; left fingers follow the chopping hand, supporting its wrist. Eyes on blade. (Fig. 20)

Remember: While crouching, left leg is crossed over the right with sole of foot on ground, and right heel is off ground with buttocks sitting on right shank. While chopping, right arm is fully extended lower forward, keeping blade of sword parallel to ground. The chopping and crouching should be completed at the same time.

21A

Form 8   Lower Tap with Knee Raised
1. Right hand holding sword turns hollow down, keeping sword level and flat, and both legs straighten on balls of feet, turning torso backward from right, while right hand draws a horizontal circle with sword. As sword comes back to right side of body, torso leans back to left, and the blade swings on upward in an arc until sword point is beside right ear; then left fingers are raised on left side with elbow bent. Eyes looking down in front. (Fig. 21A)

21B

2. Following the preceding step, right leg stands erect, raise left knee bent, and torso bends to right side while right hand taps forward with sword, thumb on top. Eyes on sword point. (Fig. 21B)

Remember: Leaning back to swing sword outward and raising knee with tapping forward the sword top should be well coordinated and completed at the same time. Right leg should stand straight with left knee drawn as high as possible. While tapping, right wrist should bend down. Making sword, arm, left arm, and pointing fingers all pointing on the same vertical spot.

22A

Stage Three

Form 1 Straight Thrust with Feet Together
1. Torso turns backward from left on ball of right foot. Meanwhile, right arm twists inward with wrist bent and sword beside body, pointing forward: left fingers swing down before right shoulder and abdomen in an arc before pointing out straight forward with hollow of hand downward. Eyes on pointing fingers. (Fig. 22A)

22B

2. Drop left foot forward, and the right follows up close beside it, bending both legs in a sitting position. Meanwhile, right hand holding sword thrusts straight forward with thumb on top; left fingers come naturally beside right wrist. Eyes on sword point. (Fig. 22B)

Remember: Both thighs must be level while sitting with knees and feet close together. Torso is inclined forward with back straight and bottom suspended. Both arms are extended with shoulder in line with sword point.

23

Form 2   Raise Sword with Bow Step

Right foot takes a step forward, bending knee, while left heel turns inward slightly, stretching left leg taut to form a right bow step. Right hand raises sword pointing straight up with hollow of hand facing left; left fingers remain pointing forward with hollow of hand downward. Torso is slightly inclined forward, eyes on pointing fingers. (Fig. 23)

Remember: Left arm is extended straight with shoulder swung forward and fingers slightly above shoulder; the right is raised erect with edge of blade facing forward. Throw out chest with back straight and waist arched.

24

Form 3   Chop with Cross-Legged Crouch

Right leg stands erect, and left foot takes a step forward with toes turned out, crossing legs before they bend deep at knees in a crouch. Meanwhile, right hand chops down forward with sword, thumb on top and sword point at ankle level; left fingers stick to the inside of right wrist. Torso is bent forward with eyes on sword point. (Fig. 24)

Remember: The same as in Form 7, Stage Two

25

Form 4   Reinforce Wrist (Right)

Both legs partly straight up on balls of feet, turning torso right, and right leg is half crouched with the left slightly bent, ball of foot on ground, forming a left hollow step. Right arm twists inward, turning thumb downward and drawing an upward arc with lower edge of blade, then as torso is raised to form a hollow step, right hand is drawn up backward on right with left fingers still stuck to wrist and both elbows slightly bent. Eyes on front end of sword. (Fig. 25)

Remember: Weight must be fully rested on right leg with torso slightly inclined forward and sword held horizontal above the right of forehead, sword point slightly higher than handle.

26

Form 5   Reinforce Wrist (Left)

Left foot takes half a step forward, turning torso backward from left on ball of foot, and the right also takes a step forward with ball of foot on ground. Both legs are partly bent with weight center on the left and in a right hollow step. As right foot steps forward, right arm twists outward swinging sword left and forward in an arc with hollow of hand on top and blade parallel to ground; left fingers then clear away from right wrist to be raised above with elbow bent. Eyes on front end of sword. (Fig. 26)

Remember: The same as in Form 4.

27A

Form 6 Hop and Flip
1. Left foot takes a long step forward, and the right is immediately drawn off ground behind with shank. Meanwhile, right hand swings outward with sword up to left and hollow of hand turned inward, elbow bent, until the sword is on left side of body with hand over left hip, thumb on top and wrist turned up; left fingers are laid on right wrist as it comes down on left side. Eyes on sword point. (Fig. 27A)

27B

2. Left foot stamps ground, and as soon as the right foot hops to right, landing with knee bent and squatting slightly, the left is drawn off ground with knee bent behind to right to keep balance while torso is bent towards left. As right foot hops off ground, right hand swings sword down to right in an arc, and when it comes to the right of body, right arm twists outward, but with a flick of wrist flips sword upward; left fingers are raised on left side with arm extended horizontally and elbow bent, thumb downward. Eyes looking right. (Fig. 27B)

Remember: The hop and flip of sword must be well coordinated and done swiftly. In flipping sword, the wrist must jerk up hard. To keep balance, right leg should bend slightly at knee, and left shank should be drawn as high as possible. Torso is twisted right, and sword is raised obliquely above the right of forehead and held slack so as to enable the wrist to turn up.

28A

Form 7   Press Down with Side Crouch
1. Right hand swings sword point back over head to right in horizontal arc, and when it comes to the right of body, draws back sword with handle before chest, elbow bent and hollow of hand upward. Meanwhile, right leg stands erect holding torso upright, and left knee is drawn up in front with left fingers still across upper left of forehead. (Fig. 28A)

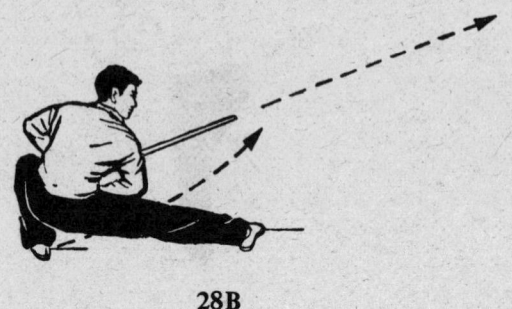

28B

2. Following the preceding step, left pointing fingers drop in front to rest upon right wrist. Left foot lands, taking a side step to left fully crouched; right leg is stretched horizontally with toes turned in, forming a right side-crouch. Meanwhile, right hand presses sword down flat, pointing up obliquely to right. Torso is inclined forward, eyes looking right. (Fig. 28B)

Remember: While crouching sideways, left leg must be completely crouched with bottom against heel and not jutting up, both feet flat on ground. Throw out chest while torso is inclined forward with both arms crooked, forming a circle.

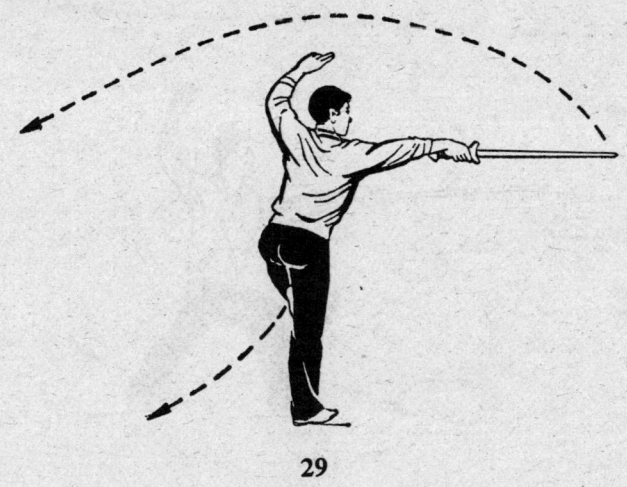

29

Form 8 Straight Thrust with Knee Raised

Both legs stand up, and left leg is drawn up in front with knee bent, while the right stretches erect. Meanwhile, right hand holding sword thrusts straight forward with thumb on top; left fingers are raised on left side with elbow bent, forefinger down. Eyes on sword point. (Fig. 29)

Remember: Right leg should be held erect and firm, with left knee drawn as high as possible and back of foot held taut, toes pointing straight down. Torso is inclined slightly to right with right shoulder and arm in line with sword and left arm crooked in a half-circle.

30

Stage Four

Form 1   Side Cut with Bow Step

Right arm twists outward, turning hollow of hand backward and lower edge of blade up, and then torso turns left. Meanwhile, left foot takes a wide side step to left, bending knee; right foot turns heel slightly out on ball of foot, and right leg stretches taut, forming a left bow step. Left fingers follow the movement of right arm, going right, down, left and up in a circle, ending again raised above head on left side with arm bent; meanwhile, right hand cuts forward horizontally with sword, thumb on top, arm extended and sword point slightly above shoulder. Eyes on sword point. (Fig. 30)

Remember: The forward cut and circle drawn by pointing fingers must be well coordinated and completed at the same time, with both shoulders relaxed.

31

Form 2   Back Cut
Right foot takes a step forward with knee slightly bent; left foot is drawn off ground with shank upward, and torso is inclined forward and twisted clockwise at waist. Right hand cuts back with sword, as right foot steps forward, pointing obliquely down, thumb down; left fingers are extended sideways slightly upward, thumb down. Eyes on sword point. (Fig. 31)
Remember: Right leg must stand firm with black of left foot drawn taut. Chest is thrown out with shoulders relaxed.

32A

Form 3　　Flip with Cross-Legged Crouch
1. Right foot stamps ground, and left foot jumps forward ahead, turning torso backward from right; left foot lands with toes slightly turned out, and right leg is swung behind. While torso turns right, right arm twists clockwise turning thumb on top; left fingers are fully extended backward horizontally with hollow of hand downward. Eyes on sword point. (Fig. 32A)

32B

2. Following the preceding step, right foot lands behind of body, and both legs crouch fully with knees bent, left over right, and bottom rested on right shank, forming a cross-legged crouch. Meanwhile, right hand holding sword presses down with arm straight, wrist turned up and sword pointing up; left fingers are raised above head on left side with arm bent, forefinger downward. Eyes on blade. (Fig. 32B)

Remember: The hop, crouch and flip of sword should be well linked up. The leap must be wide and light, landing with ball of foot first. The wrist should jerk up hard in flipping sword, keeping sword point level with brow. While crouching, torso is bent forward with chest in.

33A

Form 4   Side Cut with Bow Step
1. With left toes turned inward, torso turns about clockwise, and right foot immediately takes a step forward, with left leg stretched taut, forming a right bow step. Right arm twists outward, turning hollow of hand upward, as torso turns right, right hand holding sword is drawn before left ribs with elbow bent; left fingers then drop in front upon sword handle. Torso is inclined forward; eyes looking forward. (Fig. 33A)

33B

2. Following the preceding step, right hand holding sword slashes upper forward in an arc with hollow of hand obliquely upward and wrist partly turned in; meanwhile, left fingers point backward extended, with thumb on top. Eyes on sword point. (Fig. 33B)

Remember: While slashing, right arm is kept lower than shoulder with sword pointing up to right in front and sword point a little higher than head; left arm is fully extended horizontally behind with finger tips a little above shoulder.

34A

Form 5   Step Up with Left Cut
1. Right leg is straightened, and torso turns left with left knee bent. Meanwhile, right hand turns in an arc, passing before face and the side of body to left with hollow of right hand turning inward. Sword to left. As the sword comes in front, left fingers are laid upon right wrist. Eyes on sword point. (Fig. 34A)

34B

2. Torso turns backward from right on right heel with toes turned outward; left foot then takes a step forward with ball of foot on ground. Right hand holding sword with backhand to cut down, forward and up in an arc, ending with sword up in front at shoulder level, with elbow slightly bent and thumb down; left fingers following right hand remain on right wrist. Eyes on sword point. (Fig. 34B)

Remember: The sword must be swung forth and back in a complete circle. On swinging up sword, right leg is slightly bent, while the left is straightened with weight shifted on the right and sword pointing slightly downward.

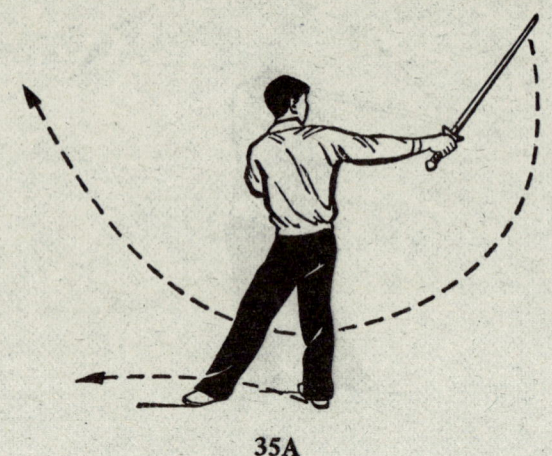

35A

Form 6   Step Up with Right Cut
1. Right hand swings sword in an arc upward and then backward to right obliquely, and left fingers are drawn before right shoulder with hollow of hand facing leftward. Eyes on sword point. (Fig. 35A)

35B

2. When left foot is well set on ground, turn its toes out on heel, and right foot takes a step forward in front of the left with toes on ground. Meanwhile, right hand swings sword in an arc downward and forward, ending with elbow slightly crooked, hollow of hand upward and sword point upward levelly with head; left fingers come down in front and go up behind in a circle until it is raised above head on left side with elbow bent. Eyes on sword point. (Fig. 35B)

Remember: The same as in Form 5, only with left and right reversed.

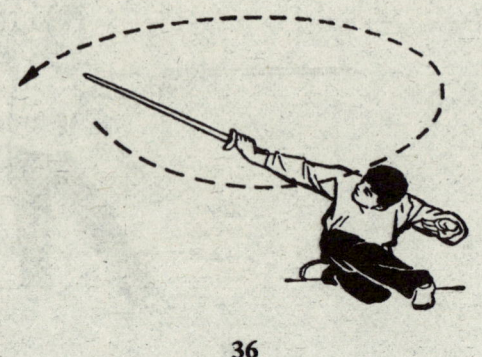

36

Form 7   Back Cut with Cross-Legged Squat

Right foot is set flat on ground before taking a small step forward, and the left takes a side step to right behind the right before both legs crouch crossed in a squatting position. While left foot is stepping to right, right hand swings sword up, left, then down and back and to right and upward again in a circular curve, ending with sword point above head; left fingers drop past front of body, draw an arc upper backward, ending beside left ear with arm extended sideways bent at elbow, thumb down. Torso is bent forward to left. Eyes on sword point. (Fig. 36)
Remember: The squat must be well coordinated with swinging sword. While squatting, left leg is curled with left side of foot on ground; right leg is curled over the left with sole on ground and toes pointing forward. Torso is bent forward with chest in and sword point in line with right arm, left elbow and shoulder.

37A

Form 8   Horizontal Swirl

1. Right foot treads ground to make both legs straighten upright, turning torso backward from left on balls of feet; then right leg crouches a little with foot well set on ground, and left leg is bent slightly with ball of foot on ground, shifting weight on the right leg. Meanwhile, right hand swings sword in a circle with elbow bent to keep sword holding levelly, thumb down as torso turns about; left fingers are laid upon right wrist. Eyes on sword point. (Fig. 37A)

37B

2. Following the preceding step, torso immediately leans back, and right hand swings sword to left, back, right and forward in a horizontal circle until sword is in front of body with hollow of hand upward and handle loosely held, making sword point to tip down; open left hand with thumb on top, ready to take over sword from the right. Weight is then shifted forward, and left foot is well set on ground with right leg straightened erect and torso inclined forward. Eyes on left hand. (Fig. 37B)

Remember: Turn of torso should be well linked with swirl of sword, and the latter should be done horizontally and swiftly with a flexible wrist.

38

Closing Stance

Form A

Right hand passes over sword to left hand and turns into point-fingers, left hand closes over cross-piece to hold sword with handle downward perpendicularly on left side. Then right foot takes a step forward obliquely to right with toes turned in and leg slightly crouched, torso turns naturally left; left foot then is shifted forward with ball of foot on ground and knee slightly bent. As torso turns left, right pointing fingers are raised from behind body above head on right side with elbow crooked and hollow of hand upward. Eyes are looking to the left horizontally. (Fig. 38)

Remember: Weight is shifted on right leg with torso inclined forward, chest out, back arched, shoulders relaxed, left elbow slightly tucked up, blade against back of forearm, perpendicular to ground.

39.

Form B

Straighten right leg erect, bring right foot together with the left to stand straight. Right pointing fingers drop on the side of body with hollow of hand downward to return into the Opening Stance. Eyes are looking straight ahead. (Fig. 39)
Remember: The same as in Opening Stance.

Chapter Two
ELEMENTARY BROADSWORD-PLAY

1. List of Forms

Opening Stance

Stage One

1. Swirl Around Head with Bow Step
2. Hide Sword with Hollow Step
3. Forward Thrust with Bow Step
4. Swing Up with Feet Together
5. Left Cut
6. Right Cut
7. Side Parry with Bow Step
8. Hide Sword with Bow Step

Stage Two

1. Swirl Around Head with Knee Raised
2. Horizontal Cut with Bow Step
3. Swing Back with Side-Crouch
4. Cut Down with Cross-Legged Crouch
5. Left Overhead Cut
6. Right Overhead Cut
7. Press Sword with Cross-Legged Crouch
8. Cut Back in Horse-Ride Stance

Stage Three

1. Low Cut with Bow Step
2. Cut Back from Below with Cross Step
3. Turn, Thrust and Cut Downward
4. Cut Downward with Side-Crouch

5. Poise Sword and Forward Thrust
6. Left Oblique Cut
7. Right Oblique Cut
8. Hide Sword with Hollow Step

Stage Four

1. Swirl and Sweep Around
2. Turn Over and Cut Downward
3. Swirl Around Head with Hop-Kick
4. Press Sword with Side-Crouch
5. Swirl around Head and Kick Up
6. Hide Sword with Hollow Step
7. Swirl around Head with Bow Step
8. Hand Over Sword with Feet Together

Closing Stance

2. Instruction on Techniques

1

Opening Stance

Stand erect with both feet together, eyes looking straight forward. Hold sword in left hand with handle upside-down, blade in front, tip pointing upward, back of blade against inside of forearm, and guard against wrist; right hand hangs down on right side with fingers extended together. (Fig. 1)

2A   2B

Form 1
1. Right hand is raised fully extended from the side in an arc with palm facing left. (Fig. 2A)
2. Right arm twists clockwise with elbow crooked, and comes down before left shoulder near left armpit with palm facing up; at the same time, left hand holding sword come in front with elbow bent inside right arm, and is raised fully extended with hollow facing right, sword pointing down. Eyes on right hand. (Fig. 2B)

 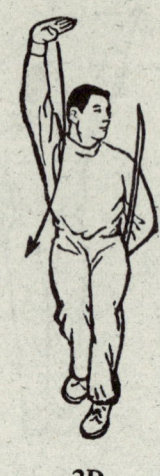

2C   2D

3. Right hand swings down and right in an arc, and the left holding sword comes down on left side in an arc. Eyes follow right hand. (Fig. 2C)

4. Right hand moves on upward until it is overhead with wrist bent, palm horizontally facing forward, and elbow slightly crooked; left hand holding sword goes on down in an arc until it is behind back with forearm slightly raised, hollow of hand facing right. As right hand is raised, right leg bends into a half-crouch, and left foot moves forward with ball of foot on ground, knee slightly bent. Eyes looking left. (Fig. 2D)

Remember: All the movements should be linked up without break. In a hollow step, weight must rest fully on the crouched leg, with chest out and back arched.

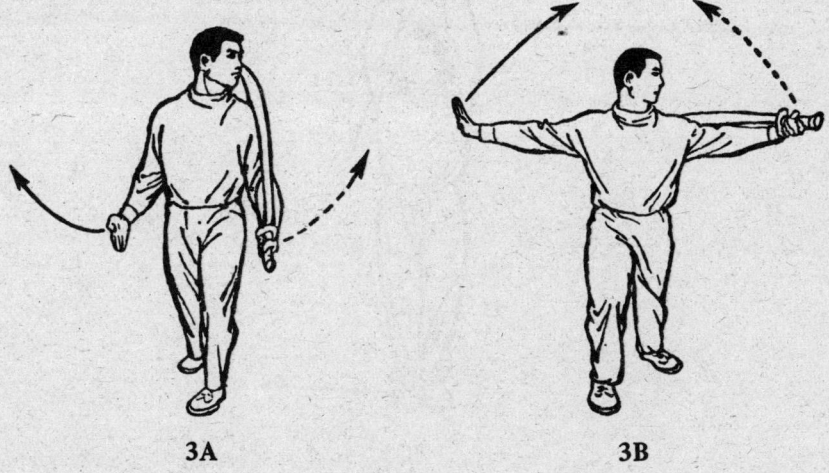

3A   3B

Form 2
1. Left foot takes half a step forward with knee slightly bent. Right foot remains in position, stretching right leg straight. At the same time right palm goes down behind in an arc with arm held in obliquely. (Fig. 3A)
2. Right foot takes a step forward with knee slightly bent. Left foot remains in position, stretching leg straight. Left hand holding sword extends sideways simultaneously with the right in a "T" position. (Fig. 3B)

3C

3. Right leg stands erect, and left foot comes together with the right. Left hand holding sword with the right making an arc to meet above forehead with right thumb on guard of sword, ready to take over handle from left hand. (Fig. 3C)

Remember: Movements of feet ahead should be well coordinated with the movement of arms until the hands meet.

4A

Stage One

Form 1 Swirl around Head with Bow Step
1. Right leg crouches a little, and left foot takes a step to left. Right hand swirls sword anti-clockwise around with back of blade close to body, and left arm twists clockwise with thumb facing downward, and extends to left, palm facing backward. Eyes looking left horizontally. (Fig. 4A)

4B

2. Torso turns left, stretching right leg straight, and left leg bends into a left bow step. At the same time, right hand holding the sword with hollow turned up. Torso turns left, and swings sword from behind to right, forward and left in a horizontal circle, ending under left armpit with hollow of hand turned down, back of blade against left ribs, and tip pointing horizontally backward; left arm is then raised with elbow bent and palm lying horizontal over head. Eyes looking straight forward. (Fig. 4B)

Remember: While swirling, back of blade should be held close to spine. As it sweeps out, the blade must be held level and swung out swiftly.

5A

Form 2   Hide Sword with Hollow Step
1. Torso turns right, stretching left leg straight, and right leg bends at knee. With the turn of torso, right hand turns hollow down and swings sword right horizontally, ending with back of blade facing forward; left palm comes down tended to left, facing up. Eyes on blade. (Fig. 5A)

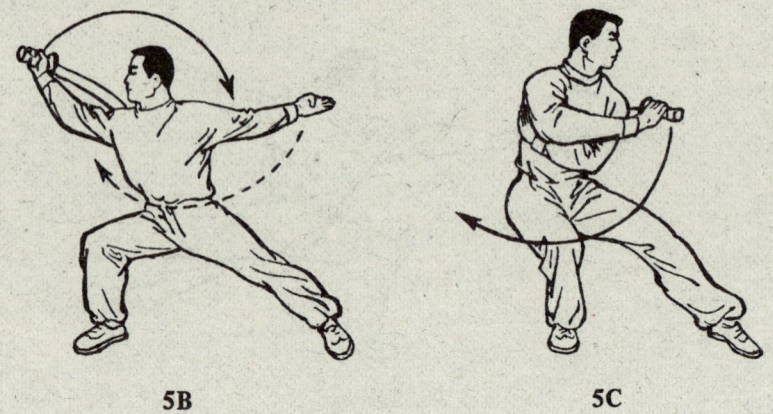

5B 5C

2. Right arm twists clockwise with the stroke, turning hollow of hand up with back of blade swung behind horizontally. (Fig. 5B)

3. Right heel turns out on ball of foot, and torso turns left. Left foot takes half a step backward with knee slightly bent, and right leg is slightly crouched. Right hand swings sword to left from behind towards left shoulder, pointing downward; meanwhile left hand swings before body under right armpit in an arc. Eyes looking left. (Fig. 5C)

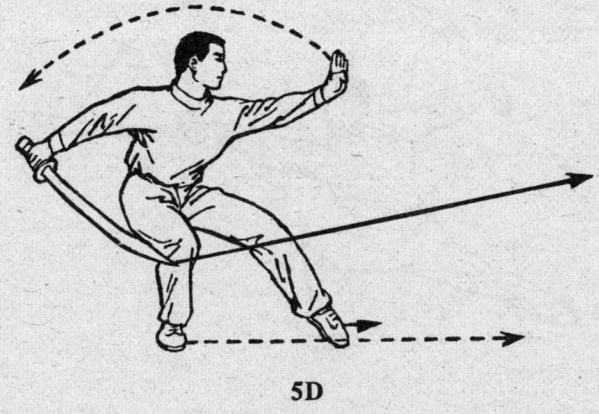

5D

4. Right leg is half crouched, and left leg remains slightly bent with ball of foot barely touching ground, shifting weight fully on to the right in a hollow step. Right hand goes on swinging sword down and backward with elbow slightly bent, tip pointing forward, blade facing down; Left palm is held erect with small finger foremost, and pushes forward, fingers pointing up. Eyes on left palm. (Fig. 5D)

Remember: The movements should be well linked up. The sword must be swung horizontally, and in swirling, the back of blade must be held close to spine.

6

Form 3   Forward Thrust with Bow Step

Left foot is shifted forward a little and set firm on ground, and the right takes a step forward with knee bent, while left leg stretches straight, forming a right bow step. At the same time, left palm goes up and back with arm extended in an arc, ending in a hooked hand behind pointing down; right hand holding sword lunges forward with blade facing down. Eyes on sword tip. (Fig. 6)

Remember: Sword point must be in line with right hand and shoulder with torso inclined forward.

7

Form 4   Swing Up with Feet Together

Left foot remains in position as weight is shifted back, and right foot treads back to withdraw beside the left and stand fully erect with it. Meanwhile, right hand holding sword swings up backward, and with a flick of wrist turns sword down behind back with back of blade against spine; left hooked hand swings to left horizontally at shoulder level. Eyes looking straight forward. (Fig. 7)

Remember: Throw out chest with back and legs straight, left arm stretched levelly and right elbow slightly crooked.

8A 8B

Form 5 Left Cut

1. Left foot remains in position, and the right takes a step forward obliquely to left. At the same time, right hand holding sword cuts down in front obliquely to left, and left hooked hand opens into a palm supporting right elbow. Eyes on blade. (Fig. 8A)
2. As sword comes down, right arm twists anti-clockwise, and with a flick of wrist turns sword tip backward behind body; weight is shifted gradually forward. (Fig. 8B)

8C 8D

3. Right foot remains in position, and the left takes a step forward obliquely to left, bending left knee with right leg stretched straight to form a left bow step. Right hand holding sword is raised with blade facing up and left palm still laid on right elbow. (Fig. 8C)
4. Right hand cuts down in front obliquely to right with sword tip slightly turned up; left arm at the same time is raised with elbow bent and palm laid across forehead. Eyes on sword tip. (Fig. 8D)

Remember: Swinging up and down must be well linked up, done with force, and coordinated with footwork.

9A   9B

Form 6   Right Cut

1. Right leg is partly crouched, and weight is shifted onto right leg with left leg slightly crooked. Right hand withdraws sword to right below with blade facing down. (Fig. 9A)
2. Right hand swings on sword, twisting arm clockwise, and going down, to right with back of blade facing up. Meanwhile, left palm comes down in front before right shoulder in an arc. (Fig. 9B)

9C   9D

3. Right leg stretches straight, and left foot takes a step forward obliquely to right. Left palm swings left in an arc, and right hand raises sword with arm twisted clockwise and blade facing up. (Fig. 9C)
4. Right foot takes a step forward obliquely to right, bending knee, and left leg stretches straight, forming a right bow step. Right hand holding sword cuts down in front obliquely to left with tip of blade held slightly upward; left palm swings to left and up in an arc until it is raised above head horizontal with arm crooked. (Fig. 9D)

Remember: The same as in Form 5.

10A

Form 7   Side Parry with Bow Step
1. Right hand turns blade up with a clockwise twist of arm; point-forward, and right foot is raised off ground. (Fig. 10A)
2. Right foot lands in front. Right hand swings sword up, backward and down close to body in an arc, while left palm comes down to rest upon back of blade. Eyes on sword tip. (Fig. 10B)
3. Left foot takes a step forward, bending leg in a half-crouch, and right leg stretches straight into a left bow step. At the same time, right hand swings sword forward turning blade slanting up with tip pointing down; left palm remains on back of blade with fingers pointing up. Torso is inclined fully forward, eyes on tip of sword. (Fig. 10C)

Remember: Swinging of blade must be coordinated with footwork.

10B

10C

11A

Form 8　Hide Sword with Bow Step
1. Right hand swings sword horizontally backward with hollow down, and left arm is extended horizontally on left side. (Fig. 11A)
2. Torso turns right with left toes turned in, and right foot takes a step back stretching straight, while the left is bent at knee. Right arm twists clockwise as sword is swung behind with back of blade leading and tip pointing down. (Fig. 11B)
3. Left foot takes a step back obliquely to left, stretching leg straight, and right leg is bent at knee. Meanwhile, left palm comes down under right armpit in an arc, and right hand swirls sword around back beyond left shoulder. (Fig. 11C)

11B

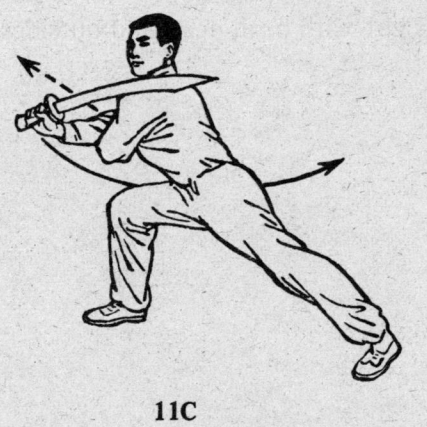

11C

11D

4. Right leg half crouches to form a right bow step. Right hand draws sword back from outside left shoulder down to right with blade down and tip pointing forward; left palm swings out and pushes forward, facing left, with fingers pointing up at eyebrow level. (Fig. 11D)

Remember: Swirl sword swiftly. Sword is hidden close behind right thigh which is held level with tip beside knee. Left leg is stretched straight with both heels and outsides of feet well set on ground.

12A 12B

Stage Two

Form 1 **Swirl around Head with Knee Raised**
1. Right foot remains in position, and the left takes a step forward. Left palm is drawn back before right shoulder with elbow bent, and right hand swirls sword around left arm to left and behind with tip pointing down. (Fig. 12A)
2. Left toes turn out, and torso turns left. Right hand swirls on sword around left shoulder toward spine, and left palm is swung left horizontally with arm extended. (Fig. 12B)

12C

3. Left foot remains in position with leg erect, and right knee is raised in front with back of foot taut and toes pointing down. Right hand swings sword out from behind and with an anticlockwise twist of arm, swings sword horizontally under left ribs with back of blade against them and tip of sword pointing backward; left palm is raised from left, facing up with arm crooked over head. Eyes looking right. (Fig. 12C)
Remember: The standing leg must be held erect; right knee should be raised as high as possible with sole close to the crotch Torso is held erect, and right arm is held close to but not against chest.

13

Form 2   Horizontal Cut with Bow Step

   Left foot remains in position, and right foot lands to right, turning torso right slightly with left leg stretched straight and the right half crouched in a right bow step. Right hand swings sword forward horizontally with hollow downward, aiming at opponent's mid section, and tip pointing forward; left palm drops back with arm extended and fingers pointing backward. Eyes are looking at the tip of the sword. (Fig. 13)
Remember: The blade must be held level when cutting, and tip of sword should be in line with wrist and shoulder.

14A

Form 3   Swing Back with Side Crouch
1. Right arm turns outward with blade up, tip of sword pointing down obliquely. (Fig. 14A)

14B

2. Left leg is fully crouched with toes out slightly and right leg is stretched straight over ground with toes turned in, forming a side-crouch. Right hand swings sword back to left in an upward arc with arm bent, blade remaining upward and tip still pointing down obliquely; left palm meanwhile is laid on inside of handle with arm crooked and thumb downward. Eyes looking right. (Fig. 14B)

Remember: Turning blade and swinging back must be linked up. While side-crouching, heels and outsides of soles should not be off ground, and torso is inclined slightly to left.

15A

Form 4   Cut Down with Cross-Legged Crouch
1. Torso is raised slightly. Right hand swirls sword behind from right shoulder to left with tip pointing down; left palm is extended horizontally to left at the same time, with thumb downward. (Fig. 15A)

15B   15C

2. Right foot remains in position, and the left takes a side step to right from behind. Meanwhile, left palm comes down in an arc from under right armpit; right hand swirls sword over left shoulder with hollow downward. Blade held levelly, pointing backward. Eyes are looking to the right. (Fig. 15B)

3. Both legs are fully crouched crossed, right over the left, with sole of right foot and ball of the left on ground, and the buttock sitting on left shank. While squatting, right hand cuts down in front to right with blade facing downward obliquely and tip of sword pointing forward; left palm then swings up to left and is raised horizontal above head, with elbow bent. Eyes on blade. (Fig. 15C)

Remember: All above movements must be well linked up. While cutting down, force is concentrated on second half of blade.

16A

Form 5 Left Overhead Cut
1. Stand up and both legs still crossed. Draw left palm back in front of right brow, supporting on right wrist; right hand swings sword in an arc from outer part of left arm to the left with sword tip downward. (Fig. 16A)

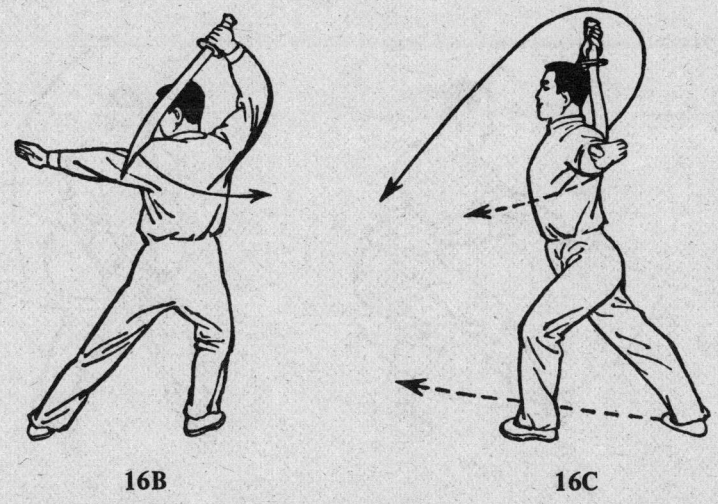

16B   16C

2. Torso turns about counter-clockwise on balls of feet. Left palm swings left horizontally with thumb downward; right hand swirls sword around spine. Right knee bent slightly. (Fig. 16B)
3. Torso goes on turning left to form left bow step. (Fig. 16C)

16D   16E

4. Left foot remains in position, and the right takes a step forward obliquely to left with right knee slightly bent. Right hand swings sword forward overhead obliquely from back to left, with tip pointing obliquely down; left palm then supports right elbow with arm bent, fingers pointing upward. (Fig. 16D)
5. Following the cut, right arm twists counter-clockwise with elbow bent, swinging sword back with blade downward; left palm is now laid on right wrist. Eyes are looking to the left. (Fig. 16E)

Remember: Turning, Swirling, and cutting must be swiftly linked up.

17A   17B

Form 6   Right Overhead Cut

1. Torso is partly raised, and turns right. Right hand raises sword overhead with tip pointing downward, swinging sword back around left shoulder and with back of blade close to spine, and then left palm is raised overhead too. (Fig. 17A)
2. Left foot takes a step forward obliquely to right, and bend right leg slightly. Meanwhile, right hand cuts down from the backside of body to the front, then the right side (outside right leg) with sword pointing obliquely down; press left palm on right wrist. (Fig. 17B)

17C

3. Following the cut, right arm twists clockwise with elbow bent, swinging sword up behind with blade downward, and left palm is then separated. Eyes on tip of sword. (Fig. 17C)

Remember: The cut must be done swiftly with force.

18A

Form 7   Press Sword with Cross-Legged Crouch
1. Right arm twists clockwise with elbow bent, turning blade up with tip of sword downward, and right hand swirls sword behind back from right to left. Eyes on right hand. (Fig. 18A)

18B   18C

2. Left heel turns out on ball of foot, and the right takes a side step from behind to left. Right hand goes on swinging sword around left shoulder, and meanwhile, left palm is raised to rest on inside of right wrist. (Fig. 18B)
3. Both legs are fully crouched, left over right, with sole of left foot and ball of the right on ground, bottom sitting on right shank. Right hand presses sword down to left, and left hand rests on right wrist, with blade down and tip of sword pointing backward. Eyes on blade. (Fig. 18C)

Remember: The side step, crouch, swirl and press must be linked up swiftly.

19A   19B

Form 8   Cut Back in Horse-Ride Stance

1. Both legs kick slightly against the ground to stand up, and torso turns about. Meanwhile, both hands are raised on left side with tip of sword pointing downward. Eyes on tip of sword. (Fig. 19A)
2. Both legs half crouch into a horse-ride stance. Right hand swings sword back to right with tip of sword held slightly upward at eyebrow level; left palm is raised above head with arm bent, facing up. Eyes on tip of sword. (Fig. 19B)

Remember: The turn and cut should be swift. In horse-ride stance, toes of both feet should be turned in, and both thighs levelly.

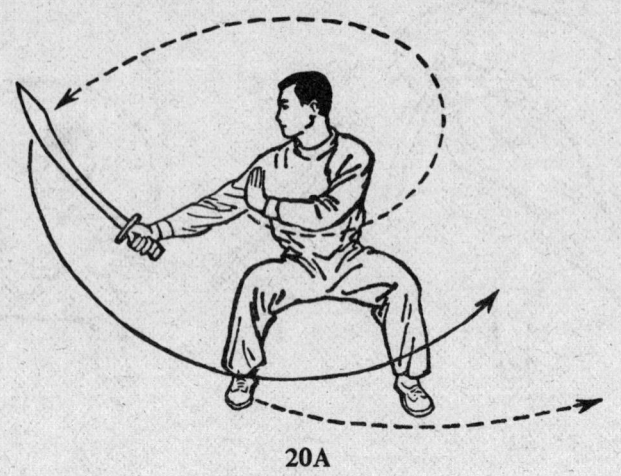

20A

Stage Three

Form 1   Low Cut with Bow Step
1. Left palm goes in an arc from above to the front of right shoulder. Eyes are looking at left palm. (Fig. 20A)

20B

2. Torso turns left, and right foot takes a big step to left side, bending left knee with left leg stretched straight. Meanwhile, left palm swings down to left and up in an arc, ending raised obliquely behind the body, palm facing upward, and right hand swings sword up to left side with blade upward and tip pointing obliquely downward. Eyes on tip of sword. (Fig. 20B)

Remember: The stepping forward should be done simultaneously with the low cut.

21A

Form 2   Cut Back from Below with Cross Step
1. Torso turns left, and right stretches straight with the left knee bent. Meanwhile swing right hand archwise from right, upright and backside of body, left palm is drawn back before right side of chest with elbow bent. Eyes follow sword. (Fig. 21A)

21B

2. Torso turns right, and left foot takes a side step to right side from behind. Right hand goes on swinging sword down and right back with blade obliquely upward; left palm pushes out to left with arm bent slightly, thumb downward and fingers pointing obliquely forward. Eyes on sword tip. (Fig. 21B)

Remember: The above movements should be well linked up, and torso is slightly inclined forward while taking side step.

22A   22B

Form 3   Turn, Thrust and Cut downward

1. Torso turns about counter-clockwise on balls of feet. With a flick of wrist, right hand turns sword tip up, and with the turn of body, thrusts sword up with blade in front and tip pointing up to right; left palm turns with body. (Fig. 22A)
2. Torso goes on turning left backward, crossing legs with the left before right. Revolve right hand archwise from upward, downward and then the left with turning of upper body; left palm presses on right wrist with elbow bent. Eyes on sword tip. (Fig. 22B)

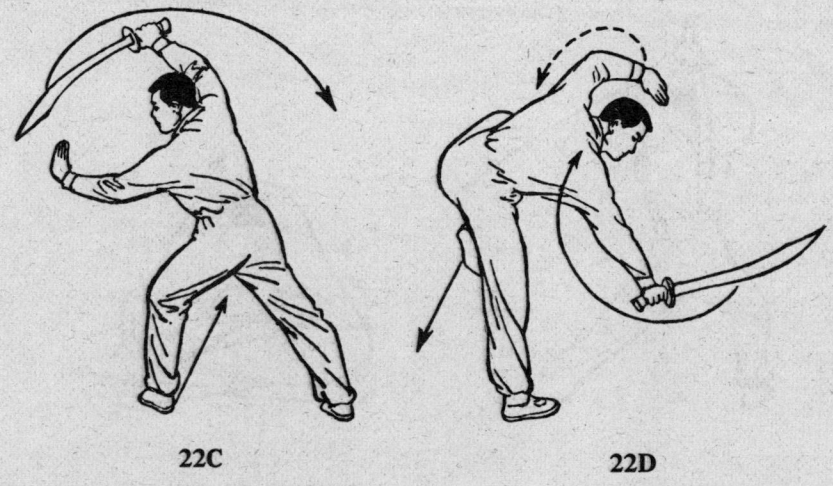

22C   22D

3. Left foot remains in position, right foot takes a side step to right. Right arm twists inward, raising up the sword with blade upward; left palm makes an arc from right wrist downward, then left extending horizontally. (Fig. 22C)
4. Right leg stands erect, and left leg raise with knee bent before abdomen and torso inclined to right. At the same time right hand cuts down to right with force, blade downward, sword tip slightly pointing upward; left palm is then raised above head, facing forward with elbow bent. Eyes on sword tip. (Fig. 22D)

Remember: In thrusting sword up, right wrist must be turned up to avoid tip of sword touching ground. The thrust should be well linked with the cut, and stand firm on one leg.

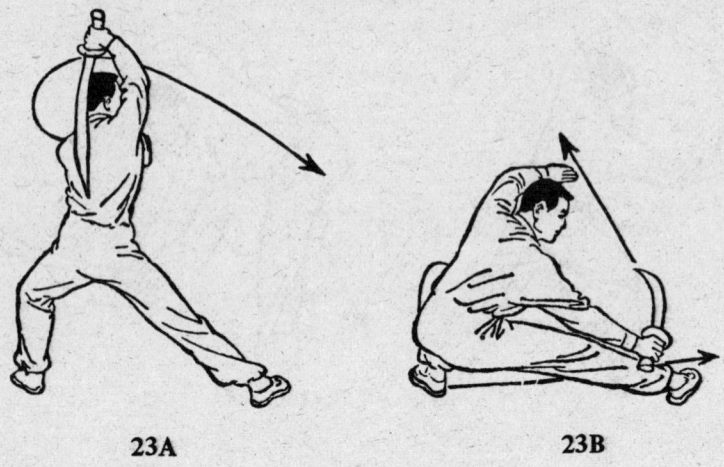

23A　　　　　　　　23B

Form 4　Cut Downward with Side Crouch
1. Left foot lands on left side, bending left knee, right leg stretching straight. Right hand twists clockwise with elbow bent, turning blade backward with tip downward, and swirls sword from outer side of the right shoulder around head to left; meanwhile, revolve left palm archwise from upward, left, downward and to the front of right chest with palm erect, fingers pointing upward. (Fig. 23A)
2. Left leg crouches deep, the right stretches straight in a side-crouch. Right hand cuts levelly from behind to left, forward and then lower right with blade facing right and tip pointing forward; left palm is held horizontal above head with elbow bent. Eyes on blade. (Fig. 23B)

Remember: While cutting, force is concentrated on second half of blade.

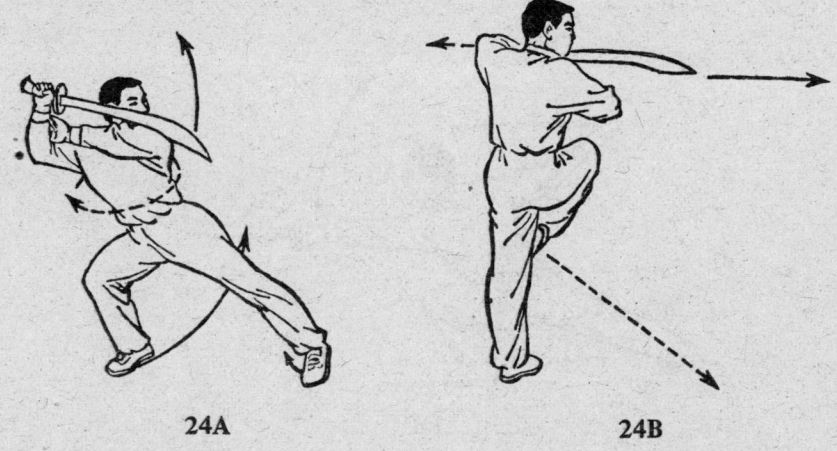

24A   24B

Form 5   Poise Sword and Forward Thrust

1. Left foot treads the ground to stand up and takes a step to right, and torso turns about clockwise with right knee bent slightly. Right hand raises sword and twists counter-clockwise, turning blade up; meanwhile, left palm is laid on right wrist near thumb. Eyes looking forward. (Fig. 24A)
2. Torso turns about clockwise on ball of left foot with right knee drawn up. While turning, right hand raises sword with the leg over head, keeping sword in the same direction; on turning, both arms bend to lower blade horizontally, which is still facing up, pointing in same direction as it is now poised over right shoulder. (Fig. 24B)

24C

3. Right foot lands in front, and left leg is stretched straight as the right bends into a right bow step. Right hand thrusts sword straight forward with blade downward, while left palm is extended to left in a "T" position with fingers pointing backward slightly upward. Eyes on tip of sword. (Fig. 24C)

Remember: All the above movements must be swiftly linked up. While turning, tip of sword remains pointed at the same object.

25A

Form 6   Left Oblique Cut
1. Torso turns about clockwise on balls of feet. Right hand twists counter clockwise, turning sword tip down, and swirls sword from left shoulder towards spine behind; left hand swings in an arc to outer side of left shoulder. Eyes on left hand. (Fig. 25A)

25B 25C

2. Bend left knee and draw it up. Right hand swings sword around head and cuts down in an arc from behind, right, front to lower left; left palm rests on right forearm with torso inclined slightly forward. (Fig. 25B)
3. Following the cut, right arm twists inward with right wrist, swinging sword to left backward, pointing slightly upward. (Fig. 25C)

Remember: Stand firm while drawing up left knee, and cut down swiftly with force.

26A   26B

Form 7   Right Oblique Cut
1. Drop left foot forward. (Fig. 26A)
2. Torso turns backward from right, right knee raising up from ground. Right hand swings sword around and cuts down obliquely from left, forward to lower right, and left palm is extended to left pointing obliquely upward. Eyes on tip of sword. (Fig. 26B)

Remember: The same as in Form 6.

27A   27B

Form 8   Hide Sword with Hollow Step
1. Drop right foot backward and erect, left leg bent. Right hand meanwhile twists clockwise with wrist turned up, and swings sword up around back from right to left. (Fig. 27A)
2. Weight is shifted backward with right leg partly crouched, left foot takes half a step back. Right hand swings sword from behind around outer side of left shoulder, while left palm comes down in an arc to right armpit. (Fig. 27B)

27C

3. Right hand draws sword downward, back to right with elbow slightly crooked, blade downward and tip pointing forward; left palm is held erect and pushes straight out with fingers pointing upward. Meanwhile, right leg is half crouched and the left leg bent, forming a hollow step with weight on the right. Eyes on left palm. (Fig 27C)

Remember: While swirling sword, keep back of blade close to spine. When hiding sword, right wrist should be turned up, keeping tip of sword up and not drooping down.

28A

Stage Four

Form 1   Swirl and Sweep Around
1. Left foot stands firm on ground. Right hand with arm twists inward, turning tip of sword down, and swirls sword along left arm toward left shoulder, and left palm is laid upon right wrist near thumb with arm bent. (Fig. 28A)

28B   28C

2. Left toes turn out and right foot takes a step forward, turning torso left. Right hand swings sword from left shoulder to right, while left palm swings to left fully extended. Eyes are looking to the right. (Fig. 28B)
3. Left foot takes a right side step from behind, and right hand swings sword around outer side of right shoulder. Eyes on right hand. (Fig. 28C)

28D　　　　　　　　　　28E

4. Both legs fully crouch crossed, and right hand with hollow down swings sword down forward from outer side of left shoulder in a quick sweep. Eyes on blade. (Fig. 28D)
5. Torso turns about backward from left, and right hand swings sword along in a low sweeping circle. Then both legs stand upward. Following the sweep, right hand turns hollow downward and lay blade against outside of left arm; left palm is laid on right wrist near thumb. (Fig. 28E)

Remember: The low sweep must be done very swiftly, holding blade level and low.

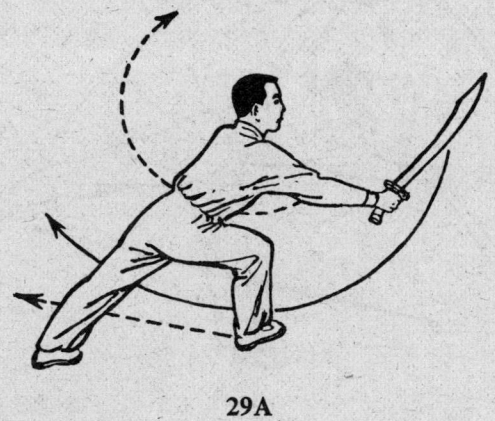

29A

Form 2   Turn Over and Cut Downward
1. Torso turns right while right hand swings sword overhead to right, and left palm is laid on right forearm. Eyes on tip of sword. (Fig. 29A)

29B

2. Right foot swings of ground to left, and the left hops up, while torso turns about backward from left in the air, landing on right foot forward. Meanwhile, left palm swings down in a circle to left, backward and up, ending in a horizontal position over head with arm bent; with the turn of body, right hand swings sword down to left and backward in an arc with blade turned up. Eyes on right hand. (Fig. 29B)

29C

3. Torso goes on turning backward. Left foot lands with a side step to right behind, and left leg is fully crouched with the right stretched straight, forming a side-crouch, while torso is inclined forward obliquely to right. On landing of left foot, right hand swings sword in a circle overhead and cuts down; left palm swings down, backward and up again, ending raised horizontal over head with elbow bent. Eyes on tip of sword. (Fig. 29C)

Remember: The jump may be long but not high, and the cut should describe a semi-circle.

30A　　　　　　　　　　30B

Form 3　Swirl around Head with Hop-Kick

1. Left foot stands, raising torso erect. Left palm is drawn before right shoulder with elbow bent, and right hand twists inward, keeping tip of sword pointed downward, and swirls sword around left shoulder towards spine. Meanwhile, left foot swings up, and right foot kicks against the ground to leap up. Left palm swings to left horizontally. (Fig. 30A)
2. While in the air, right hand swirls sword around head from behind to right, then goes in front, ending under left arm pit in a circle; left palm is raised over head, lying horizontal with elbow bent. Meanwhile, right foot treads ground with heel to kick forward, and left foot then lands on ball of foot. (Fig. 30B)

Remember: The swirl and hop-kick must be well coordinated, the former done swiftly and the latter with force by a straight leg.

31A 31B

Form 4   Press Sword with Side-Crouch
1. Torso turns right, right hand swings sword to right, and cutting backward obliquely down, while the left is raised obliquely upward with palm facing upward. Eyes on blade. (Fig. 31A)
2. Right leg is drawn back with knee bent. Right hand twists clockwise, turning tip of sword down, and swings sword from right shoulder towards spine. Eyes looking to the right. (Fig. 31B)

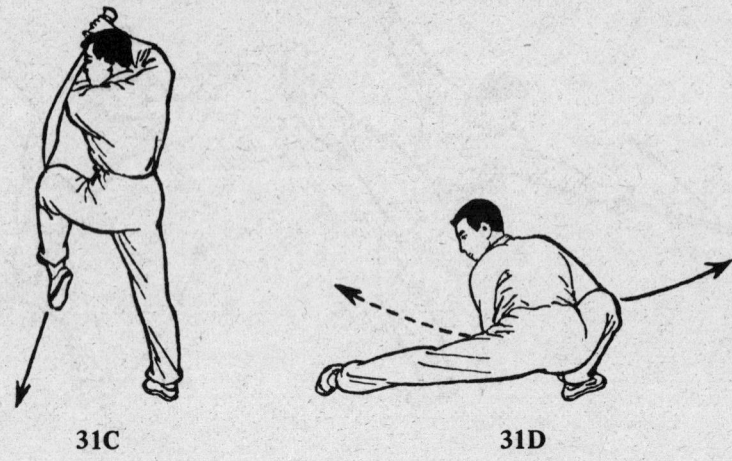

31C   31D

3. Torso turns backward from right, and left foot treads ground to jerk up, right foot drops on ground. While hopping, right hand brings sword close around left shoulder, and left palm is laid naturally on right wrist near thumb. (Fig. 31C)
4. Right leg is fully crouched, and left foot lands on left side with leg stretched straight, forming a side-crouch. Right hand presses sword down with the aid of the left which still remains on right wrist, keeping tip of sword pointed to left and blade downward. Eyes looking left. (Fig. 31D)

Remember: The right back cut should be swift with force, so that the hop and about turn will come after it with ease. In crouching, left toes should turn in with outsides of both feet and heels on ground, and torso inclined forward to left.

32A   32B

Form 5   Swirl around Head and Kick Up
1. Right leg stands erect, with left knee drawn up. Right hand draws sword back to right, and left palm is extended forward to left with fingers pointing up. Eyes on left hand. (Fig. 32A)
2. Torso turns left, and right hand swings sword around below left knee and up from left, while left palm is laid upon right forearm with elbow bent. Eyes looking down in front. (Fig. 32B)

        32C   32D

3. Right hand swings sword around left shoulder towards spine, and left foot lands in front obliquely to left, while left palm swings horizontally to left with palm turned downward. (Fig. 32C)
4. Left leg is half crouched, and the right is stretched straight forming a left bow step. Right hand swings sword around from back, right shoulder and body to left armpit in a circle, ending with arm turned over and back of blade against left ribs, left palm is raised overhead in a horizontal position with elbow bent. (Fig. 32D)

32E

5. Right foot turns toes up and kicks upward in front with heel. Eyes on toes. (Fig. 32E)

Remember: The swirl of sword must encircle left knee and shoulder besides head and should be done quickly, the kick must be swift, following the swirl of sword closely.

33A

Form 6   Hide Sword with Hollow Step
1. Right foot lands in front. (Fig. 33A)
2. Left foot hops forward with the right off ground, and torso turns backward from right. With hollow of hand downward, right hand sweeps a complete horizontal circle with sword around body, and left palm swings from upward to left backward, palm facing upward. (Fig. 33B)
3. Right foot lands backward, and right hand twists outward, swinging sword from right shoulder towards spine. (Fig. 33C)

33B

33C

33D   **33E**

4. Left palm goes down from left side to right armpit in an arc and is then laid on right wrist while right hand swings sword over right shoulder from behind. (Fig. 33D)
5. Right leg is half crouched, and the left is slightly bent with ball of foot on ground, forming a left hollow step. Right hand withdraws sword downward with tip pointing forward; left palm pushes straight forward with fingers pointing upward. Eyes on left palm. (Fig. 33E)

Remember: The hop, turn and landing must be well coordinated with sweep and swirl of sword.

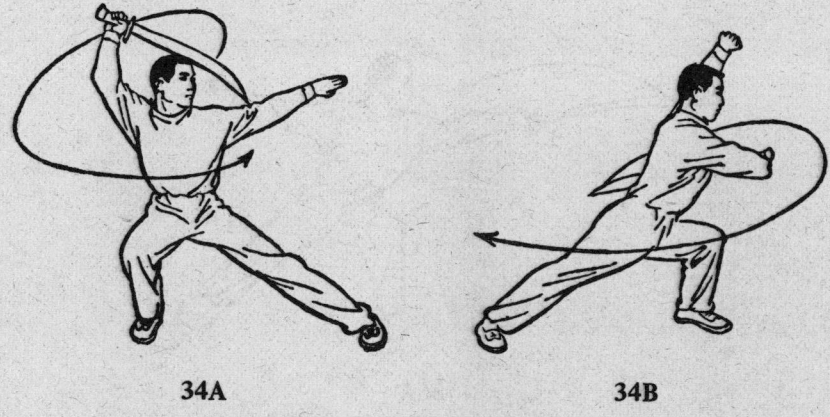

34A   34B

Form 7   Swirl around head with Bow Step

1. Left foot takes half a step forward obliquely to left, stretching leg straight. Meanwhile, right hand twist anti-clockwise, turning tip of sword down, and swings sword around left shoulder towards spine. (Fig. 34A)
2. Right leg is stretched straight and the left is half crouched forming a left bow step. Right hand swings sword around right shoulder and body to left armpit in a circle, ending with arm turned over, back of blade against left ribs, and tip of sword pointing backward; while, left palm is raised overhead in a horizontal position with elbow bent. Eyes looking forward. (Fig. 34B)

Remember: While swirling, keep back of blade close to spine, and sweep sword around swiftly.

35A

Form 8 Hand Over Sword with Feet Together
1. Left leg is stretched straight, and the right is bent while torso turns right. Right hand sweeps to right horizontally with sword, and left palm swings left horizontally, facing up, in a "T" position. Eyes on tip of sword. (Fig. 35A)

 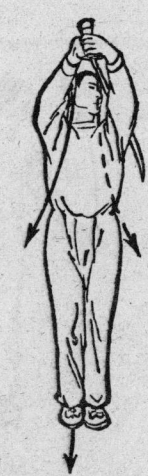

35B   35C

2. Following the sweep, right hand turns outward, swinging sword back horizontally. Eyes on right hand. (Fig. 35B)
3. Right leg stands erect, and left foot comes together with right. Right hand raises sword handle above forehead with tip down, blade backward; meanwhile, left palm is also raised above forehead with thumb out and hollow over handle, ready to take over sword from right hand. Eyes are looking to the right. (Fig. 35C)

Remember: The closing step should be coordinated with hand-over of sword.

36A   36B

Closing Stance

Form A
1. Left hand takes over sword and drops in front with the right each to one side, and left hand holds sword upside down with back of blade against arm, blade facing forward and tip pointing up. Left foot takes a step back. (Fig. 36A)
2. Right foot takes another step backward. Meanwhile, right palm swings back and up beside right ear in a horizontal position, facing forward with thumb down; left hand holding sword remains in position. Eyes on right hand. (Fig. 36B)

37

3. Left foot steps back beside the right, standing erect. Right hand drops in a pressing position, facing down with elbow crooked outward a little; left hand holding sword remains in position. Eyes looking left. (Fig. 37)

Remember: The stepping back should be swiftly linked up with back swing of arm.

ISBN 962-238-003-4
Zuijiuquan
— A Drunkard's Boxing
(Chinese-English)
by Cai Longyun & Shao Shankang

Zuijiuquan is a pictographic boxing in Chinese Martial Arts. As the name connotes, it contains movements depicting a person in a drunken state. With its unique and fantastic movements, this veritable heirloom has been handed down from generation to generation.

Zuijiuquan helps strengthen muscles, improve the flexibility of joints and the elasticity of ligaments, and anhance the functional co-ordination between the feeling, the nerve and the muscles. It is also beneficial to the internal organs, such as those of blood circulation and respiration. Therefore, *Zuijiuquan* is a good exercise for fitness building.

The author, Mr. Cai Longyun is now the associate professor and head of the *Wushu* teaching and research section of the Shanghai Institute of Physical Culture, and concurrently vice-Chairman of the Chinese Wushu Association. And Mr. Shao Shankang is now the leader and coach of the Shanghai Wushu team, member of the Chinese Wushu Association, deputy director of the Coach Committee of the Chinese Wushu Association and Secretary-General of the Shanghai Wushu Association.

162 pages   *14.5 x 21 cm.*   *Paper*